Success

Great Little Book on Mastering Your Time

By
Brian Tracy

CAREER PRESS
3 Tice Road, P.O. Box 687
Franklin Lakes, NJ 07417
1-800-CAREER-1; 201-848-0310 (NJ and outside U.S.)
FAX: 201-848-1727

Copyright © 1997 by Brian Tracy / Reprinted by permission of Successories®, Inc.

All rights reserved under the Pan-American and International Copyright Conventions. This book may not be reproduced, in whole or in part, in any form or by any means electronic or mechanical, including photocopying, recording, or by any information storage and retrieval system now known or hereafter invented, without written permission from the publisher, The Career Press.

SUCCESSORIES®: GREAT LITTLE BOOK ON MASTERING YOUR TIME
Cover design by Jenmar Graphics
Typesetting by Eileen Munson
Printed in the U.S.A. by Book-mart Press

To order this title by mail, please include price as noted above, $2.50 handling per order, and $1.50 for each book ordered. Send to: Career Press, Inc., 3 Tice Road, P.O. Box 687, Franklin Lakes, NJ 07417. Or call toll-free 1-800-CAREER-1 (NJ and Canada: 201-848-0310) to order using VISA or MasterCard, or for further information on books from Career Press.

Library of Congress Cataloging-in-Publication Data

Tracy, Brian.
    Great little book on mastering your time / by Brian Tacy.
      p.   cm. -- (Successories)
    ISBN 1-56414-329-5 (pbk.)
    1. Time management.   I. Title   II. Series.
HD69.T54T7   1997
640'.43--dc21   97-39487
                                                                   CIP

The quality of your *life* is determined by the quality of your time management.

ଔ☉ଓ

Time is your most precious resource, all you have to *trade* for the things you want in life.

ଔ☉ଓ

Time is perishable; it cannot be saved. It can only be *spent* in different ways.

Time is irreplaceable; nothing else will do, especially in relationships.

ଔ☺ఴ

Time is indispensable; all work requires an expenditure of time.

ଔ☺ఴ

Time is essential for accomplishment of all kinds. How are you using yours?

Time management is a *skill* that can be learned with discipline and practice.

ॐ🕐ॐ

Time management enables you to control the *sequence of events*.

ॐ🕐ॐ

You are always free to choose what you do *first,* what you do *second,* and what you do *not at all.*

Time management requires *self-discipline*, self-mastery, and self-control more than anything else.

୧✦୨

Time management is really personal management, life management, and management of *yourself*.

Most people engage in activities that are tension-relieving rather than *goal-achieving*.

03 🕐 80

Continually ask yourself if what you are doing is your highest ROTI—"Return on Time Invested."

03 🕐 80

Your ability to manage your time for maximum results is the *core skill* of personal effectiveness.

Time is the raw material of life. How are you processing *yours?*

అంఁఎ

Don't complain of having too little time; you have *all the time* there is—24 hours each day.

అంఁఎ

High productivity comes from *leveraging* your time by doing *only* the most important things.

Develop *long-time perspective* in your life; where do you want to be in five years?

☙🕐❧

Your ability to *delay gratification* in the short-term will determine your financial success in the long-term.

The *value* of anything can be determined by how much of your time you are willing to *trade* for it.

All fortunes begin with the sale of *personal services,* the sale of personal time.

The worst use of time is to do *very well* what *need not* be done at all.

Doing what you really *enjoy* is the key to peak performance.

൦ଓ🕐ଓ൦

"Whenever you find something getting done, you find a monomaniac with a mission."
—Peter Drucker, management speaker and author

Happiness comes when you *believe* in what you are doing, *know* what you are doing, and *love* what you are doing.

છ☼ૹ

Is there anything in your life that, knowing what you *now* know, you wouldn't get into today?

Practice *creative abandonment* with those activities that are no longer important to you.

સ‍🕐🥧

Keep asking: "What is the *most valuable use* of my time right now?"

સ‍🕐🥧

Time management is a *vehicle* to take you from wherever you are to wherever you want to go.

What are your *core values* in life? Are your goals and activities consistent with these values?

ଔ🕑ଛ

What are your *three* most important goals in life right now? Are you allocating your time accordingly?

How would you change your life, what would you do differently, if you won $1 million cash today?

What would you do, how would you spend your time if you learned today that you only had *six months to live?*

What are your dreams? What would you like to be, have, and do if you had *no limitations?*

ය☼ෑ

What one great thing would you dare to *dream* if you knew you could not fail?

ය☼ෑ

What is your *personal mission?* Are you living your life consistent with it?

Continuous learning is the *minimum* requirement for success in your field. Learn something new every day.

ଓଃ☉ଥ

Every action (or inaction) involves a *choice* between what is more important and what is less important.

The Law of the Excluded Alternative says that doing one thing means *not* doing something else.

ༀ☉ༀ

The Pareto Principle, the *80/20 Rule*, says that 20 percent of your activities will account for 80 percent of your results. What are your top 20 percent?

Set both priorities and *posteriorities* on everything you do. What activities should you *discontinue* to free up more time for those activities that are truly important?

∞🕐∞

The Law of Forced Efficiency says that there is always enough time to do the *most important things*.

The key determinant of priorities should be the long-term potential *consequences* of an activity.

ය⊙ৡ

What are the most important things you do, measured by their *long-term* consequences?

ය⊙ৡ

What can you, and only you do, which, if done well, will make *a real difference*?

Your rewards will always be determined by your results; what *results* are expected of you?

 C8🕐80

"Action without thinking is the cause of every failure."
—Alex McKenzie, time management expert

In managing your time, your *happiness* should be your chief aim in life.

03🕐80

To do more of one thing you must do less of something else. What should you be doing more of? Less of?

Treat your time like money; how can you best *spend* it to achieve maximum satisfaction?

ೞ☉ಐ

Set *peace of mind* as your highest goal and organize your time and life around it.

ೞ☉ಐ

Small improvements in the way you use your time can translate into major differences in your life.

When you work, *work all the time you work*; put more of yourself into what you do.

ଔ☉ଛ

When you are with your family, *be there* 100 percent of the time—emotionally as well as physically.

To get more time with your family, limit and restrict television, newspapers, and outside activities.

ଔ☉ର

Spend unbroken *chunks of time* with the most important people in your life.

ଔ☉ର

It's *quantity* of time at home and *quality* of time at work that counts; don't mix them up!

If successful people are both effective and efficient, they do the right things and they do them right.

അ⏰ഌ

With excellent time management, you get more *living* out of life, more time for the people and things you enjoy.

In developing excellent time management skills, focus on changing only *one behavior* at a time.

०ऽ⊙४०

No matter what you have done to this moment, you get 24 brand-new hours to spend every single day.

०ऽ⊙४०

It doesn't matter where you're *coming from*; all that matters is where you're *going*.

"Our great business is not to see what lies dimly at a distance, but to do what lies clearly at hand."
—Winston Churchill

ɞ🕐ʅ

Focus and concentration are the keys to high performance.

ɞ🕐ʅ

Clear, specific *goals* are absolutely indispensable to success and achievement.

What do you want in life? What do you really, *really* want?

෨☉౦

What are your *highest-value* activities? Work on *these* exclusively.

෨☉౦

Why are you on the payroll? What *specifically* have you been hired to accomplish?

What one skill, if you developed it and did it in an excellent fashion, would have *the greatest positive impact* on your life?

∞🕐∞

Your rewards in life will be determined by *what* you do, *how well* you do it, and the *difficulty* of replacing you.

The Law of Sowing and Reaping is the basic principle of human life. You are reaping today the result of what you have sown in the past.

03️⃝80

One of the best uses of your time is to *increase* your competence in your key result areas.

03️⃝80

To earn more you must *learn* more.

You are maxed out today at your *current* level of knowledge and skill.

ଔ☉ଈ

The future belongs to the *competent*.

ଔ☉ଈ

Continuous personal and professional development is your *key* to the future.

What are your *core competencies?* What are the essential skills that enable you to do your job well today?

ଔ 🕐 ଓ

The better you get at your key skills, the more you accomplish in a shorter period of time.

What are your unique talents and abilities? How could you leverage them to the maximum?

ᘓ☉ᘔ

What is your personal *area of excellence?* What could it be?

ᘓ☉ᘔ

Your life only gets better when *you* get better.

You are where you are and what you are because of yourself, because of your own choices and decisions.

ଔ☉ଔ

Everything counts! Everything you do either helps you or hurts you; nothing is neutral.

ଔ☉ଔ

The starting point of making *better* choices is for you to stop making *worse* choices.

What are the critical success factors of your job? What must you be absolutely, positively excellent at doing to be successful?

ଔ☉ଓ

What are your areas of major strength and weakness? One weakness is all it takes to hold you back.

What is your *limiting step*? What is the one key skill or ability that determines your level of success?

 os⊙so

What can you do, starting *today*, to overcome your weaknesses and maximize your strengths?

os⊙so

Take all the *training* you can get; one good idea is all you need to save yourself years of hard work.

Read in your field at least one hour per day. This habit will eventually make you one of the most knowledgeable people in your business.

ᦏ 🕐 ᦐ

Turn your car into a *learning machine* by listening to educational audio tapes as you drive.

Your aim in time management is to increase your *Return on Energy*, for you to get more *living* out of life.

ଓ 🕐 ଈ

Every minute you spend in planning saves 10 minutes in execution; this gives you a 1,000-percent *Return on Energy*!

Use a "to-do" list to plan your work. Write everything down before you begin.

ಣ☉೩

Use a time planner as your central organizer; think on paper.

ಣ☉೩

Plan every week the week before, every day the day before.

Save time by having everything you need at your fingertips before you begin a major task.

ぐ⏰ぞ

Complete your tasks one at a time. Whenever you are finished with something, put it away.

ぐ⏰ぞ

The core personal productivity habit is *neatness*. Important tasks are not entrusted to messy people.

Practice *single-handling* with every task. Once you begin, stay at it until it's complete.

ℤ⏰Ω

Discipline yourself for maximum productivity by repeating "back to work!" over and over.

ℤ⏰Ω

Practice the *body language* of high performance. Sit erect and lean forward into your work.

Use the 30-Percent Rule—always allow a cushion of 30 percent to complete any major tasks.

‌‌‌‌‌‌‌‌‌‌‌‌‌‌‌‌ ⊗🕐⊗

Lack of clarity is the number-one time-waster. Always be asking, "What am I trying to do? How am I trying to do it?"

Continually *resist* Parkinson's Law, which says, "Work expands to fill the time allotted for it."

ങ⏰ജ

People can be terrible time wasters. Who wastes your time at work?

ങ⏰ജ

Whose time do *you* waste at work, and how do you waste it?

Minimize telephone interruptions; have your calls screened and held.

❧✦☙

Use the telephone as a business tool—get on and off fast.

❧✦☙

Plan each telephone call in advance. Have an agenda.

Practice the *20/80 Rule*. The first 20 percent of the time you spend planning a project will be worth 80 percent of the time you spend on the entire project.

෴☉෴

To save time with the telephone, batch your calls and make them all at once.

When you call someone, give and get a *call-back time* so you can avoid "telephone tag."

ଓଠ🕐 හ

The word "no" is a great time saver. Say *no* to anything that is not the highest and best use of your time.

Self-discipline is a great time-saver; it is the ability to make yourself work on *only* those things that are most important to you.

෴ ⏱ ෴

Use money to save time wherever possible; delegate and outsource to anyone who works at a lower hourly rate than you do.

Look upon time management as a series of skills and tools that you can use to build a wonderful life.

ඥ☺ౠ

The better organized you are in the *simple* things, the more spontaneous and free you can be in the more important things.

Lead by example. Imagine everyone around you is looking at you as a model of excellent time management.

೪☝ೕ

Visualize yourself as a good time manager; see yourself as well-organized, efficient, and effective.

Fake it until you make it. Act as if you were *already* excellent in every aspect of time management.

ଔ 🕐 ଅ

To improve your time management habits, *model yourself* after someone else who is extremely well-organized.

The ingredients of happiness are self-esteem, self-respect, and personal pride—all of which come from good time management.

ଔ🕐ଛ

See yourself as a *factory*—the purpose of time management skills is to enable you to increase the quality and quantity of your production.

For immediate improvement, start in one area in which poor time management skills are holding you back and concentrate on changing just one habit.

To develop new, positive time management habits, *launch strongly* and never allow an exception until the habit is fully entrenched.

Use the *Trial and Success* method; learn how to improve and succeed by failing and learning from your mistakes.

ങ⏰യ

Time management is a *skill*, like typing or riding a bicycle, that can be developed with practice and repetition.

The discipline of time management develops judgment, foresight, reliance, and self-discipline.

 C3 ⏲ 80

Time management skills enable you to work smarter, not just harder.

C3 ⏲ 80

Excellent time management is a source of energy, enthusiasm, and a positive mental attitude.

കൃ🕐🔊

You grow as a person according to the demands you place on *yourself*. The discipline of time management builds character, confidence, and unshakable belief in yourself.

കൃ🕐🔊

Your ability to handle *projects*, multi-task jobs, is a critical factor to your success.

⋙☜⋘

Your ability to work with others on a complex task is a critical skill for advancement at work.

⋙☜⋘

Before beginning a complex task, list every job, function, and activity that must be completed.

Start with the end in mind. What would your project look like if it were completed and excellent in every respect?

ଔ☉ଌ

What is your limiting step? What activity determines the *speed* at which your goal can be achieved?

The theory of constraints says that there is a *bottleneck* or constraint that determines the ultimate success of any project. What is yours?

ଔ☉ண

The *80/20 Rule* applies to constraints—80 percent of the reason for the failure to make progress is within *yourself*.

Practice *Crisis Anticipation* with every major goal: Ask, "What can possibly go wrong?"

෪🕐෨

Errant assumptions lie at the root of every failure. What are yours?

Remember that *Murphy's Laws* apply to everything you do:

- ⏱ Everything takes *longer* than you expect.
- ⏱ Everything costs *more* than you originally plan.
- ⏱ Whatever can go wrong, will go wrong.
- ⏱ Of all the things that can go wrong, the worst possible thing will go wrong at the worst possible time and cost far more than you ever expected.
- ⏱ Murphy was an optimist.

Instead of trying to do several things at once, focus on doing one thing at a time and doing it right.

ᑲ☽☉☾ᑭ

You are only as free as your well-developed *options*. Always have a fallback plan or alternative in case your first plan doesn't work.

Make every minute count. Use *gifts of time* when traveling and between meetings to read, learn, and grow.

⋐🕐⋑

Keep asking yourself, "Is what I'm doing right now contributing to the accomplishment of my most important goals?"

Meetings are a necessary business tool and you must do everything possible to maximize the time spent in them.

ଓଟ୍ର

Always have a clear, written agenda for every meeting and every participant.

ଓଟ୍ର

Start and stop meetings on time. Assume the late-comer is *not* coming.

Time is the currency of the 90s and beyond. Always be looking for ways to reduce the amount of time required for any task.

ঙ🕐ছ

Reorganization—continually seek better, faster, more efficient ways to accomplish the same result.

Reengineering—process analysis. Look for ways to simplify the process and reduce the number of steps in accomplishing any result.

 glyph glyph glyph

Restructuring—continually look for ways to focus your time and resources on the few things that contribute the greatest value to your company and your customers.

Reinventing—look continually for ways to completely change what you are doing so that your activities are more congruent with your long-term goals.

CB🕐BO

Indecision is a major time waster; 80 percent of decisions should be made the first time they come up.

Delegate everything you possibly can so that you have enough time to do the few things that only you can do.

လ⊙ဆာ

Before starting a task, ask yourself, "Does this *have* to be done, at all? Does it have to be done *now*? Does it have to be done *by me*?"

Fast tempo is essential to success. Develop a "bias for action" in everything you do.

ଓଓ

Develop a reputation for speed and dependability to get onto the "fast track" in your career.

ଓଓ

Discipline yourself to be punctual; don't keep people waiting.

Delegate decision-making whenever possible. "When it is not necessary to decide, it is necessary *not* to decide."

❧ 🕐 ☙

The *Law of Comparative Advantage* says that you should assign, delegate, or have someone else do any job that can be done at a wage less than you earn or desire to earn.

If you want to earn $50,000 per year, you must earn $25 per hour. Ask, "Would I pay someone else $25 per hour to do what I'm doing right now?"

There are many things that you can no longer afford to do. Always ask, "Who can do this cheaper than me?"

To get more done, start a little *earlier*, work a little *harder*, stay a little *later*.

ങ☉ക

Increase your productivity by working faster. Develop a sense of urgency and get on with it!

ങ☉ക

Batch your tasks; do all of the same tasks at the same time.

Get on the *learning curve*. The more you do of the same thing, the less it takes you to complete each additional task.

ೞ🕐ೱ

Make fewer mistakes. Do it *right* the first time.

ೞ🕐ೱ

Simplify your work. Reduce the number of steps necessary to complete any task.

Do fewer things but *more important things* to increase your productivity.

ೞ☉ೲ

Do things you are *better* at. They are easier and you complete them faster.

ೞ☉ೲ

Outsource everything you possibly can. Firms that specialize do it faster and cheaper.

Make a list *before you begin* and start by deciding what you are *not* going to do.

 C3 ⊙ 80

To delegate effectively, take time to explain the task clearly.

C3 ⊙ 80

Set deadlines on all your major tasks—these act as a "forcing system" for high performance.

Practice "back from the future" thinking. Project forward *five years* and look backward.

ଔ☺ଷ

Design your *ideal* lifestyle. What would you have to do more of or less of to create it?

ଔ☺ଷ

When you ask other people to do things for you, set an order of priority on each task.

Poor or fuzzy communications are major time-wasters. Take the time to be *crystal-clear* in your communications with others.

ଔ☉ଛ

Your ability to *solve problems* efficiently and well can save an enormous amount of time.

Whatever your problem, define it clearly *in writing* before attempting to solve it.

೧⊙ಶ

Identify all the possible *causes* of a problem before you decide on a solution.

೧⊙ಶ

The *quality* of the solution you pick will be in direct proportion to the *quantity* of solutions you consider.

Whatever you decide to do, develop *a fall-back position* in case that doesn't work.

ឰ⊙ຂ

Practice *anticipatory thinking.* What is *likely* to happen and what will you do then?

ឰ⊙ຂ

Avoid *reverse* delegation; don't let people delegate the task back to you.

By delegating clearly, you can multiply your output by moving from what you *can do* to what you *can control*.

ദ്ദ⏰ജ

Assign to others *everything* that can possibly be done by them.

Taking time to *teach others* how to do a task is a major time-saver for you.

☞⊙☜

If someone can do the task 70 percent as well as you, delegate it to them and stand aside.

Salespeople work an average of 20 percent of the time, about one and one-half hours per day.

ෆ☉ෂ

Salespeople are only *working* when they are face-to-face with someone who can and will buy within a reasonable period of time.

ෆ☉ෂ

Sales success is directly proportionate to your ability to *initiate new contacts*.

Keep asking yourself, "Where is my next sale coming from?"

൭☉౭

You are in the business of prospecting, presenting, and following up. All else is secondary.

൭☉౭

Spend 80 percent of your time prospecting and presenting; spend only 20 percent of your time following up.

Ask yourself continually, "Is what I am doing *right now* leading to a sale?"

෫෯෯

Define your income and sales goals in terms of the *activities* necessary to achieve them, and concentrate on those activities.

Reduce traveling time by planning your work geographically before you set off.

03🕐80

Avoid needless perfectionism, insisting on everything being perfectly in order before beginning.

03🕐80

Take excellent care of your physical health—fatigue and illness are major time-wasters.

Go to bed *early* if you have to work tomorrow. Early to bed and early to rise is a key success principle.

ೞ☉ಬ

Invest the first hour of the day, the "Golden Hour," in *yourself*.

ೞ☉ಬ

Read 30 to 60 minutes each morning—to upgrade your skills and sharpen your intellect.

"The first hour is the rudder of the day."
—Henry Ward Beecher

ଔ☉ଊ

Schedule your first appointment early. Get up, get out, and get going.

ଔ☉ଊ

Spend your *entire day* working; make every minute count.

Two coffee breaks per day at 20 minutes each multiplied times 50 weeks per year equals 10,000 minutes or 166 hours per year. Use the time *wisely*.

ଔ☉ଔ

The average person spends one hour per day, 250 working days per year, or 250 hours per year, at lunch. Use *this* time wisely.

Superior people use their time as if *everyone* was watching, even when no one is watching.

ಅ⊙ಒ

Use a time planner continuously and write down every note and appointment.

ಅ⊙ಒ

All you really have to sell is your time—make it pay.

Your *attitude* toward your time will largely determine how much you accomplish and how high you rise.

CRUGE

The *superior* person can hold two contradictory thoughts simultaneously and still continue to function. You need a long-term vision combined with short-term focus.

Do the things *today* that will lead to the wonderful life you desire *tomorrow*.

∝☝⟩

"Self-discipline is the ability to *make yourself* do what you should do, when you should do it, whether you *feel like* it or not."
—Elbert Hubbard, author and lecturer

Save and invest 10 percent of your income throughout your working lifetime. It will make you a millionaire.

ଓଚ🕐ଅ୦

Treat your time as a scarce resource and *spend* it very carefully.

ଓଚ🕐ଅ୦

One of the biggest wastes of time in life is working at the *wrong job*. Is this the right job for you?

You will only be happy and successful when you *love* what you do and do it well.

೧🕐೩

The happiest and most productive people are doing work that they feel really *makes a difference* in the world. Are you?

೧🕐೩

Would you continue at your current job if you won $1 million cash tomorrow?

Mental flexibility is a key time management tool. How easily can you *admit* that you have changed your mind?

ఆ🕐శి

In times of rapid change, 70 percent of the decisions you make will turn out to be wrong. Admitting this is a key time-saver.

A major time-waster is staying in the wrong relationship with the wrong person. Would you get into your current relationship if you had it to do over again today?

෴☉෴

It takes character and courage to admit that you made a mistake and that you've changed your mind, but it is a major time-saver.

Set happiness as your major goal in life and organize all your activities around it.

ೞ🕐ೲ

Don't worry about what people think of you. They probably aren't thinking of you *at all*.

ೞ🕐ೲ

"If we cannot make time stand still, at least we can make it *run*."
—Christopher Marlow, English playwright

High levels of health and energy enable you to get more done in a shorter period of time.

ೞ☺ೞ

Exercise 30 to 60 minutes every day, this will keep you lean, mean and physically fit.

ೞ☺ೞ

Change your space regularly. Get up, stretch, walk around, and refresh yourself mentally.

Napping is a key time-management tool. A short nap can recharge your battery for the hours ahead.

Eat *lightly*, especially at lunch, to keep your mind clear and sharp for the entire afternoon.

Rest and relaxation are often an *excellent* use of time. They enable you to accomplish far more than you would if you were tired.

Take one full day off each week to completely recharge your mental batteries. You will get far more done in the other six days.

ఴ🕐ಐ

Take time each day to sit back, think, and reflect on your priorities so that you are using every minute well.

Time management is the one habit that is central to a satisfying, fulfilling, high-performance life.

જ⊙ဆ

Get up each morning and start work *immediately* on your biggest single task. Get it done and over with.

જ⊙ဆ

Motivate yourself by repeating the words, "Do it now! Do it now!" over and over.

Television is a major time-waster, an excellent servant but a terrible master.

 GS ⏰ ∞

Simplify your life, leave things *off* more often. Enjoy the silence.

GS ⏰ ∞

Procrastination is the thief of time, of life and of success. Resolve to overcome it.

Planning and organizing your life in advance improves your productivity dramatically.

ര⏰ഇ

Practice *Creative Procrastination* on all your activities; consciously decide *not* to do your unimportant tasks so that you have more time for your key tasks.

The Pareto Principle states that you can divide tasks into the "Vital Few" and the "Trivial Many." Which ones do you work on?

ಚಿ🕐ಭಿ

Before you begin a small task, ask yourself, "What would happened if this task were *not done* at all?"

Never give in to the temptation to clear up small things first. This can be fatal.

లు🕐ఎ

To overcome procrastination, prepare thoroughly and *list every step* of the job before you begin.

లు🕐ఎ

Do one small thing immediately—often this is all you need to do to get started.

Salami-slice your tasks—pick one small "slice" of activity and do it immediately.

రు ⊙ ఞ

Use the *Swiss cheese* method—select a five-minute part of a major task and do it *now*.

రు ⊙ ఞ

Set up a reward schedule for yourself and give yourself small rewards as you complete each part of the task.

"Procrastination is the thief of dreams."
—Cree Indian saying

ଔ☺ଷ

Develop a *compulsion to closure*. Once you begin, refuse to stop before completion.

ଔ☺ଷ

Do the task that causes you the most fear, anxiety, or stress—and get it over with.

Start from the *outside* of a large job—do several small tasks to build up momentum.

ଔ☺ଚ

Start from the *inside* of a large task—begin work on the most important job first.

ଔ☺ଚ

Visualize your major task as *completed*; see it finished in your mind's eye.

Set aside a designated 15-minute period during which you will work nonstop on your project.

ᓚᕈᖇ

Once you begin a major task, resolve to persist until it is complete.

ᓚᕈᖇ

"The first part of success is 'Get-to-it-tiveness;' the second part of success is 'Stick-to-it-tiveness.' "
—Orison Swett Marden, success author

Promise *others* that you will complete something by a certain date. Promising others motivates yourself.

❧ 🕐 ❧

"If a thing is worth doing, it is worth doing badly." —G. K. Chesterton

❧ 🕐 ❧

Anything worth doing is worth doing poorly at first. Just begin!

"Excuse-itis" is a disease that is invariably fatal to success. Avoid it at all costs.

ଔ☉ଔ

Key to success: Concentrate single-mindedly on one thing, the most important thing and stay at it until it is 100 percent complete.

ଔ☉ଔ

Every act of self-discipline in time management strengthens all your other disciplines.

The first 20 percent of a task often accounts for 80 percent of the value of the task.

ଔ🕐ଥ

Fully 30 percent of all working time is spent looking for materials that have been mislaid. File your information carefully.

ଔ🕐ଥ

Practice *completion by deletion*—eliminate all low-value tasks.

Become an unshakable optimist—look for the good in every situation.

ದಿ⊙ಸಿ

Positive, successful people think and talk about the solutions. Unsuccessful people talk about their problems. Which are you?

Information is doubling in every field every 3 to 5 years. This means your knowledge must double as well.

⋯⊙⋯

Learn speed-reading so that you can get through larger quantities of material in a shorter period of time.

Continually read, listen to audio tapes, and search for ideas that can help you to be more productive.

જ⏰ৡ

Train your memory to increase your ability to retain names, numbers, facts, and information.

જ⏰ৡ

Save time in reading magazines by ripping out the key articles and saving them in a file for review later.

Read books faster by scanning the book, front and back, before you begin reading it.

ଔ☙

Everyone today has piles of information to read, but the rule is: If it's more than six months old, it's junk!

ଔ☙

Before filing or storing anything, ask yourself if you will ever *need* this information again.

Of all information saved or filed, 80 percent is *never* referred to again.

CB⊙EO

Cut down on unnecessary reading—eliminate needless subscriptions to magazines and newspapers.

CB⊙EO

Simplify your life. Constantly look for ways to *eliminate* unnecessary tasks and activities.

"It's not the size of the dog in the fight, but the size of the fight in the dog."
—Anonymous

ༀ☉ༀ

The quality of your work is more important than the quantity.

The whole purpose of time management is to enable you to have more time to spend with the people you love, doing the things you enjoy.

ෆ☉ഃ

Coming home and going to bed *early* when you are overtired is an excellent use of time.

When you have too much to do, make a list of every single task before you begin to get your life back under control.

೫⏰ಐ

Take one day off each week, one long weekend each quarter and at least two full weeks off each year. Vacations are an excellent use of time.

Take time to think about your real goals and how you can better accomplish them every single day.

෪ 🕐 ෨

Unlock your inborn creativity. Continually look for better ways to accomplish the same task with less time and expenditure of resources.

"Do what you can, with what you have, right where you are."
—Theodore Roosevelt

ૹ⏰ૹ

When you feel overwhelmed with too much to do and too little time, remind yourself that *all you can do is all you can do*.

If you were to be called out of town for a month, what one task would you want to get completed? Begin work on that task immediately and stay with it until it's finished.

The average person wastes fully 50 percent of time at work on idle socializing and personal business. How about you?

Develop the reputation of being the hardest-working person in your company. This will guarantee your success.

ဆ🕐ဆ

Divide your desired annual salary by the 2,000 hours that you work each year in order to establish your desired hourly rate. From then on, do only things that pay that rate or higher.

ርፀ⏱ℬ

Personal development is a major time-saver. The better you become, the less time it takes you to achieve your goals.

ርፀ⏱ℬ

About the author

Brian Tracy is a world authority on time management and personal performance. He teaches his key ideas, methods, and techniques on time management to more than 100,000 people every year, showing them how to double and triple their productivity and get their lives into balance at the same time. This book contains some of the best time management concepts ever discovered.

Other best-selling audio/video programs by Brian Tracy

▶ *Action Strategies for Personal Achievement*
   (24 audios / workbook)

▶ *Universal Laws of Success & Achievement*
   (8 audios / workbook)

▶ *Psychology of Achievement*
   (audios / workbook)

To order call: 1-800-542-4252

Brian Tracy takes achievement to new heights in...
Maximum Achievement
(352 pages), Simon & Schuster

Brian Tracy's best-selling book takes 2,500 years of ideas on success and achievement and condenses them into a simple system you can use to transform your life. More than a million men and women, in 16 languages, in 31 countries, are already using Brian's powerful ideas, methods and techniques to increase their incomes, improve their relationships and unlock their potentials for happier, healthier living. This exciting book will show you how to set and achieve your goads faster than you ever thought possible. Order it today! ($12 paperback.)

To order call: 1-800-793-9552